IF FOU

MW01282091

👤 _____

✉ _____

📱 _____

Greater Than a Tourist Book Series
Reviews from Readers

I think the series is wonderful and beneficial for tourists to get information before visiting the city.

-Seckin Zumbul, Izmir Turkey

I am a world traveler who has read many trip guides but this one really made a difference for me. I would call it a heartfelt creation of a local guide expert instead of just a guide.

-Susy, Isla Holbox, Mexico

New to the area like me, this is a must have!

-Joe, Bloomington, USA

This is a good series that gets down to it when looking for things to do at your destination without having to read a novel for just a few ideas.

-Rachel, Monterey, USA

i

Good information to have to plan my trip to this destination.

-Pennie Farrell, Mexico

Great ideas for a port day.

-Mary Martin USA

Aptly titled, you won't just be a tourist after reading this book. You'll be greater than a tourist!

-Alan Warner, Grand Rapids, USA

Even though I only have three days to spend in San Miguel in an upcoming visit, I will use the author's suggestions to guide some of my time there. An easy read - with chapters named to guide me in directions I want to go.

-Robert Catapano, USA

Great insights from a local perspective! Useful information and a very good value!

-Sarah, USA

This series provides an in-depth experience through the eyes of a local. Reading these series will help you to travel the city in with confidence and it'll make your journey a unique one.

-Andrew Teoh, Ipoh, Malaysia

GREATER THAN A TOURIST- SCOTTSDALE ARIZONA USA

50 Travel Tips from a Local

Anita Shah

Cover designed by: Ivana Stamenkovic
Cover Image: https://pixabay.com/en/cactus-rocks-vegetation-arid-3810807/

CZYK Publishing Since 2011.

Greater Than a Tourist
Visit our website at www.GreaterThanaTourist.com

Lock Haven, PA

ISBN: 9781790916771

>TOURIST

50 TRAVEL TIPS FROM A LOCAL

BOOK DESCRIPTION

Are you excited about planning your next trip?

Do you want to try something new?

Would you like some guidance from a local?

If you answered yes to any of these questions, then this Greater Than a Tourist book is for you.

Greater Than a Tourist- Scottsdale, Arizona by Anita Shah offers the inside scoop on Scottsdale, Arizona and the surrounding cities, such as Phoenix, along with stops you can make in other areas of the state. These recommendations are coming straight from someone who actually lives and works there. Arizona is home to many tourist attractions, including the well-known Grand Canyon. If you are interested in going beyond the top ten attractions, experiencing wonders of Arizona and encountering lessor known gems and charms, this book is for you. Most travel books tell you how to travel like a tourist. Although there is nothing wrong with that, as part of the Greater Than a Tourist series, this book will give you travel tips from someone who has lived at your next travel destination.

In these pages, you will discover advice that will help you throughout your stay. This book will not tell you exact addresses or store hours but instead will give you excitement and knowledge from a local that you may not find in other smaller print travel books.

Travel like a local. Slow down, stay in one place, and get to know the people and the culture. By the time you finish this book, you will be eager and prepared to travel to your next destination.

TABLE OF CONTENTS

12. Goldfield Ghost Town
13. Verde Canyon Railroad
14. The Wave at Marble Canyon
15. Yayoi Kusami Firefly Infinity Mirror Room
16. Petrified National Forest
17. Strawberry Schoolhouse Museum
18. Look to the Stars at Mount Graham International Observatory
19. Beware of Pumpkin Spring Pool
20. Underground Suite, Peach Springs Grand Canyon Caverns
21. Vic & Wendy's Hot Sauce Collection, Museum, Santum, Gallery & Shrine
22. Discover an Underground Lake in Cave of the Bells
23. Watch an Old-Fashioned Shootout at the O.K. Corral
24. Her Secret Is Patience
25. Shoot Virtual Targets at Modern Round
26. Bring Out Your Inner Child at Legoland Discovery Center
27. Appreciate the History of the Apache Death Cave
28. Catch the Sunrise at Monument Valley
29. Meteor Crater
30. Grand Canyon Mule Ride
31. Flintstones Bedrock City

NOTES

DEDICATION

This book is dedicated to my loving and supportive family Jagat, Rakshak, Taran, Priya and wheaten terrier Snickers. The six of us left our home and travelled to Arizona together, settling in a place that was unfamiliar and foreign. Although climates from state to state are different, if one remains in the United States, there is always that notion that aside from the weather it can't be too different, right?

Well, after the first week of school in Arizona, it was when the weekend rolled around that my kids shared the experiences they had throughout the week. It was then that I fully realized that we were in a whole new world. They relayed to me a common rhyme that all children that grew up in Arizona were familiar with.

"Red on yellow, kill a fellow. Red on black, won't hurt Jack."

This is how to tell whether a coral snake you encounter is venomous or not. "Everyone knows this mom", they said. At that moment I realized that I needed to show them that Arizona is not all about venomous snakes and scorpions. That different can be wonderful.

Compiling the facts and recommendations needed to write this book was important to me because it is my way of showing them the beauty of Arizona. I need to thank my husband and children for being my companions in exploring this beautiful state and for knowing and showing that we lose together and we triumph together.

I am also grateful to my parents, for introducing me to Arizona during a few family vacations many years ago. It was then that I fell in love with this state and knew that one-day I would call it home.

This wonderful state is full of welcoming people, beautiful landscapes, rich history and varying cultures. People from all walks of life have settled here. I hope that my family can see Arizona through my eyes and learn to love the state as much as I do.

ABOUT THE AUTHOR

Anita Shah is a working wife and mother who currently lives in Scottsdale, Arizona and loves to vacation with her family. She grew up in the town of Des Plaines, Illinois, moved to the east coast states of Virginia and Maryland after attending college at the University of Illinois. After obtaining her Master's degree at George Washington University, she then ventured back to the Midwest with her husband and three children, to be closer to both sides of the family.

With aspirations of retiring to the state of Arizona, Anita and her husband decided to grasp an opportunity to move there a bit earlier. The couple took the plunge and headed out to the beautiful state with their three lively children and rambunctious dog. If it is good enough for retirement, it had to be good enough to move to now. The family has now settled in the lovely state of Arizona, in the proud city of Scottsdale.

Making Arizona feel like home for her family, has been one of Anita's top priorities. So, she went on a mission, to scope out unique vacation spots, find hidden gems and destinations that locals deemed

3

worthy of visiting, experience beautiful scenery and discover activities to entertain, tweens, teens and adults.

The Shahs love vacationing, new experiences and sampling great cuisine. Aside from binge watching shows on Netflix, hopping in the car, picking a direction and just exploring without a plan is one of their favorite pass times. This book is a collection of places they have discovered, fun experiences, great recommendations from locals and other splendid finds.

HOW TO USE THIS BOOK

The Greater Than a Tourist book series was written by someone who has lived in an area for over three months. The goal of this book is to help travelers either dream or experience different locations by providing opinions from a local. The author has made suggestions based on their own experiences. Please do your own research before traveling to the area in case the suggested places are unavailable.

Travel Advisories: As a first step in planning any trip abroad, check the Travel Advisories for your intended destination.
https://travel.state.gov/content/travel/en/traveladvisories/traveladvisories.html

FROM THE PUBLISHER

Traveling can be one of the most important parts of a person's life. The anticipation and memories that you have are some of the best. As a publisher of the Greater Than a Tourist book series, as well as the popular 50 Things to Know book series, we strive to help you learn about new places, spark your imagination, and inspire you. Wherever you are and whatever you do I wish you safe, fun, and inspiring travel.

Lisa Rusczyk Ed. D.
CZYK Publishing

OUR STORY

Traveling is a passion of the "Greater than a Tourist" series creator. Lisa studied abroad in college, and for their honeymoon Lisa and her husband toured Europe. During her travels to Malta, an older man tried to give her some advice based on his own experience living on the island since he was a young boy. She was not sure if she should talk to the stranger but was interested in his advice. When traveling to some places she was wary to talk to locals because she was afraid that they weren't being genuine. Through her travels, Lisa learned how much locals had to share with tourists. Lisa created the "Greater Than a Tourist" book series to help connect people with locals. A topic that locals are very passionate about sharing.

WELCOME TO
> TOURIST

INTRODUCTION

*"The world is a book, and those
who do not travel read only one
page"*

– St. Augustine

The entire state of Arizona is a gem in itself. As you arrive into the city of Scottsdale you might wonder what to do and where to venture off too. There are so many choices and many different types of vacations for visitors to experience. Are you looking for a relaxing spa of golfing getaway? Maybe staying active during your vacation is what you are looking for, so hiking, kayaking or camping is more your style. Are you escaping cold weather from another state and just want to soak in the sun? As you read through this book and while booking this trip, these are some of the questions you should be asking yourself. While I can assure you that Arizona has something for everyone, everything is definitely not for everyone.

The climate in Arizona is most probably dryer than that which you are accustomed to, so visitors will have to learn to carry water everywhere. Always carry water, even in the winter! The summers in some parts of the state are scorching hot, so tourists will learn to wear a hat, sunglasses and sunscreen. You might even see some locals walking around with umbrellas to shade themselves from the sun.

Winters in Arizona are spectacular but they can be deceiving. Winter mornings can start off with cool, but temperatures may climb 30 degrees by mid-afternoon. Wearing and carrying layers is essential. Northern parts of the state might require hats and gloves.

With wonderful weather all year around, the people of Arizona are all about nature and love to be outdoors. Creepy crawlies, javelinas, lizards and scorpions do not always linger around populated areas, but they could. If you are off exploring in the wilderness, choose function over fashion. Clothes that are made of material that provide relief from the heat and hats which provide shade are essential. Choosing closed-toed shoes over sandals and slippers are a good idea.

After you've accepted the changes, just take a moment to admire the power of mother nature, and the events and experiences that have transformed this state into a major tourist attraction. Have patience and enjoy. One trip, will not be enough to explore every part of this state. There is so much to see and so much to do. However, once you visit, Arizona will keep calling you back. So, take your time, explore, have fun and come back for more!

Although there are many things to see and many places to go, I have narrowed it down to fifty spots that I enjoy.

1. VENTURE OFF TO HORSESHOE BEND

Carved by the Colorado River into the shape of a near-perfect horseshoe, this is a sight to see. Visitors are able to walk right up to the rim and gaze upon the clear blue crystalline waters of the river that carved the attraction. With beautiful, open skies and lack of trees, there is not much shade in the area. So be certain to bring sunglasses and a hat. Sunscreen is always a good idea in Arizona.

If you just want to take in the scenery, but not touch it, catch a flight tour out of Page, Arizona for an aerial view of the area. You can fly over Horseshoe Bend and admire it from above. Beware of the parking situation though. Parking spots in Page are scarce and visitors may be asked to return at less populated time if the spots are filled up. Arriving early could be an advantage. If hiking or flying is not your thing, then try floating. A half-day rafting trip to the area can be enjoyed from the base of Glen Canyon Dam.

2. DRIVE UP SOUTH MOUNTAIN PARK

Driving up South Mountain can be quite the adventure in itself. A curvy road, winding around a mountain, with no guardrails and thousand-foot drops will make most people a little nervous. However, do not be intimidated by the narrow roads and tailgaters. Take your time and drive carefully. Although some locals or tourists may drive up the mountain quickly, I like to take my time to look around and be safe.

At the end of the paved road is my favorite nighttime view of the city lights. Just drive up about an hour before sunset and clear skies will let you see sights of Phoenix, Mesa, Camelback Mountain and surrounding cities. The view of the stars in the night sky is amazing and the city lights are just beautiful. Gazing upon the city lights at night from South Mountain is one of my fondest memories of visiting Arizona as a child, and one of the reasons I fell in love with the state.

If you want a photograph with bragging rights, go sit on the bench at Dobbins Lookout. Near the edge of the mountain, your feet will look like they are hovering in mid-air. Caution should be exercised as this is not the safest bench for little children or those with balance issues. If your vertigo is not under control you may want to avoid the bench at Dobbins Lookout.

3. TASTE SOME OF PERRY'S FRYBREAD

Do you like sampling local treats? Take a detour to Perry's Frybread stand in McNary, AZ. When following the sign to Perry's it may seem like you are pulling into the driveway of someone's home. That might be partially true, but in the heart of Navajo and Apache County, this was my first sampling of this scrumptious delicacy made of fried dough, sprinkled with sugar and served with honey.

One-hundred and fifty-four (154) years ago, the Navajo people were forced to endure the "Long Walk", to relocate from Arizona to New Mexico. Amongst other items, the government provided these Native Americans with flour, sugar and lard. These ingredients were combined and fried to make frybread. Vendors also sell frybread at concession stands near many tourist attractions, including ski resorts.

However, not only is Perry's Frybread the best, it is also sold at a much more reasonable price than the frybread sold near other attractions. Who doesn't enjoy a sweet, warm treat, especially at low prices that locals would not hesitate to pay? I would travel to Perry's over a concession stand any day.

4. SLIP & SLIDE AT THE NATURAL WATER SLIDE IN SLIDE ROCK STATE PARK

Forget about paying for admission to a water park. Slide Rock State Park offers a natural water slide that is fun for all ages. Crafted by nature, tourists will not find this attraction anywhere else. You will want to wear your gym shoes, sneakers or buy some water shoes as the sandstone rocks that lye underneath the water are very slippery. The shoes will provide some traction when you climb into or out of the water so slipping and falling will be less of a concern.

The water in Oak Creek is cool, so summer is the best time to visit this natural attraction. Park temperatures could drop to near freezing in the winter time and you do not want to take a dip at that time. As a kid I remember slipping, sliding and having a great time in this swimming hole. So, pack some towels, plastic or reusable water bottles, snacks, a change of clothes, and head out to Slide Rock State Park. Cool down and enjoy the Arizona summer.

5. EXPLORE NEW INSTRUMENTS AT THE MUSICAL INSTRUMENT MUSEUM

As a mother of three children that play the double bass in school orchestras and the Phoenix Youth Symphony ensembles, the Musical Instrument Museum is pure inspiration for music lovers. Located between Phoenix and Scottsdale the Musical Instrument Museum displays more than 6800 instruments from all around the world, including an Octobass, which is really rare, and really, really enormous!

Not only can you hear the instruments, you can also watch video displays of them being played. When you are through looking at the displays, take time to visit the Experience Gallery, which is open to guests who want to experience playing musical instruments from all different walks of life. Make sure you allow yourself ample time to peruse the different areas. Although some guests are able to view the exhibits in four to five hours, the Musical Instrument Museum could easily be an all-day event, especially if you are a musician.

6. PEAK INTO MONTEZUMA CASTLE NATIONAL MONUMENT

I love visiting places that have rich local history and tell a story. Montezuma Castle does not disappoint. Located in Camp Verde, AZ, this dwelling was built by the Sinagua Indians over 600 years ago. With five-stories and over twenty (20) rooms, it is for all purposes a prehistoric high-rise apartment complex. Supposedly, this castle took over 300 years to build.

Tours of this site are self-guided and there is a bit of walking involved so wear your walking shoes. At times, the rangers may be free to give you a mini guided tour or provide some insightful facts. If they are busy, there are still exhibits with educational information that can be read on your own. If you are visiting on a hot summer day, you may want to arrive in the early hours of the morning. An hour, or maybe two, should give you ample to peruse the area. Of course, like many other tourist attractions, there is a gift shop on the premise. I found the gift shop prices to be very reasonable and have purchased souvenirs from the shop in the past.

7. DISCOVER THE STORY OF TUMACÁCORI NATIONAL HISTORIC PARK

Located in Southern Arizona, Santa Cruz County, Tumacácori National Historic Park is home to the ruins of three Spanish mission communities, with the oldest dating back to 1691. Take a tour of Mission San José de Tumacácori, or make reservations to visit the other two missionaries. Guided tours are also available and a great way to get a history lesson from the locals.

A day trip should give you enough time to explore the church and surrounding areas. You can also hike the Juan Bautista de Anza National Historical trail near by the Santa Cruz river, or visit the Tumacácori Museum, which also doubles as a bookstore and the visitor center. Take this time to watch a brief video and learn about the area, or observe unique artifacts from that time period. If you happen to visit during the first weekend of December, the annual La fiesta de Tumacácori celebrates the numerous cultures present in the area. If you are into food stands and crafts, this could be an opportunity as there are over 50 booths for you to experience.

8. HOP IN A TRUCK TO ANTELOPE CANYON

If visiting Antelope Canyon, a gorgeous slot canyon formed by the forces of wind and water, a guided tour is the best way to go. There are two sections to this canyon, the Upper Antelope Canyon and the Lower Antelope Canyon. The Upper

Antelope Canyon is also known as "the Crack", while the Lower Antelope Canyon has been called "the Corkscrew".

Hop on a truck and be transported to the Upper Canyon. From here you merely walk in. While you admire the sandstone canyons, the tour guides do a wonderful job of explaining the local history and culture. Tours to the lower canyon are also available. The best time to visit this Canyon is during the months of March and early October. If you are a fortunate you may be able to get a glimpse of the famous light beams that shine onto the canyon, creating a wonderful illusion.

9. CAMP AT SAGUARO NATIONAL PARK

One of the first scenes that come to mind when thinking about Arizona, is that of the towering Saguaro cactus. If you want to view the largest cacti in the nation visit Saguaro National Park in Tucson. With over 92,000 acres to explore and hiking trails ranging from easy to strenuous, you can have a wide variety of experiences at this park. Orange-red sunsets are a beautiful sight.

Campgrounds are also available if you want to pitch a tent. Summer months will be hot so pack plenty of water and rations. You can also go on a 6-mile drive through the forest if you are short on time or would rather not hike. Bicycling and horseback riding is also permitted. If you do plan to make a reservation to explore on horseback please call the stables if you have children in your party. Not all stables will allow younger children to ride. A local guide can point out all the different varieties of cactus and other local flora and fauna.

10. LIGHT A CANDLE AT THE CHAPEL OF THE HOLY CROSS

Hidden away in the midst of the beautiful Sedona red rocks, the Chapel of the Holy Cross is a serene place where you can light a candle and experience the peace of Sedona. Run by the Roman Catholic Diocese, this church overlooks the Verde Valley and is beautiful in and out. It was, after all, designed by

Marguerite Straude, a student of famous architect, Frank Lloyd Wright.

Parking at the location is limited and the trek to the chapel from the lot can be quite windy and cool, even in the summer. Pack a light jacket as the feeling of calmness is well worth it. Last time I visited, admission was free. The chapel is closed during Easter, Thanksgiving and on Christmas.

11. MEET MOTHER NATURE AT HAVASU FALLS

Arizona is not all desert and cacti. Beautiful blue green waterfalls are carefully tucked away by mother nature in Supai Village of the Grand Canyon. If you want to see the Havasu Falls, plan, plan, and plan ahead. This trip is usually arranged months in advance. I would recommend you start your research one year prior to your visit.

Camping here requires a permit and 10-mile strenuous hike to the campsite. That's 10 miles each way. This is no walk in the park. The trail can be strenuous at times. Catching a helicopter to Supai

Village will cut your hike down to 2-miles each way. The view of the crystalline waterfalls is spectacular and worth the trip if you are able to make it.

12. GOLDFIELD GHOST TOWN

Do you love to experience old towns and understand how people used to live and work? Goldfield Ghost Town, reconstructed 1890's gold mining town, is located just outside of Apache Junction, Arizona. When you visit Goldfield, you will be able to take a guided tour of the underground gold mines. The tour is about 25 minutes long.

You can also ride on a narrow-gauge train, pan for gold, visit the Mystery Shack and watch an old-fashioned gun fight. If you do plan on experiencing the mine tour, train and Mystery Shack, look for a discounted admission price. Who doesn't love the Old West? Visit the Goldfield Superstition Museum to experience well-preserved history of the town. Make sure you take the kids to the ice-cream parlor and enjoy some homemade ice cream. Hot weather and ice-cream go hand-in-hand.

13. VERDE CANYON RAILROAD

Have you ever wanted to take a scenic train ride, while you sit back and relax? Verde Canyon Railroad has a four-hour train ride on a fully restored vintage train outside of Sedona, in the small town of Clarkdale. Ride 20 miles in a climate-controlled car equipped with restrooms, while you go back through locomotive history.

Fall is generally considered the most beautiful time to make this trip. The colors of trees are absolutely amazing. However, don't count out winter. If you make a reservation during the Christmas season, you will have the opportunity to travel to the North Pole and hand delivery your letter to Santa. So, make a reservation and hop on board the Verde Canyon Railroad.

14. THE WAVE AT MARBLE CANYON

Although the Wave at Marble Canyon has been around longer than any of us, it did not gain popularity until the past decade when Microsoft decided to include a picture of it as one of its desktop wallpapers. Sandstone dunes that have been frozen in time can seem a bit disorienting and vertigo inducing. However, you can't help but admire the wavelike geological formations created by erosion and wind.

This is another trip that requires preplanning. Only 20 visitors a day are allowed and a permit is required. Permits are not easy to obtain, you can apply for one or take your chance with a lottery. If you are lucky enough to get one, be prepared for the hike. You will not be surrounded by crowds so you will have the opportunity to explore in peace.

15. YAYOI KUSAMI FIREFLY INFINITY MIRROR ROOM

Outdoor activities are wonderful, but there is nothing wrong with wanting to vacation in air-conditioning. A visit to the Phoenix Art Museum is not complete until you've experienced the Yayoi Kusami Yayoi Kusami Firefly Infinity Mirror Room exhibit. Located in the Contemporary Art Wing of the museum, this exhibit will make you feel like your individuality has been erased as you immerse yourself in a room, surrounded by Kusami's Fireflies. Using lights, mirrors and a dark room, the artist has managed to create the perception that the lights are infinite, just like the universe.

If you appreciate art, you won't want to miss this exhibit, where you will also learn a bit about the artist. There are days when the museum admission is free so if you have some flexibility in when you can plan your trip, you may be able to save some money.

16. PETRIFIED NATIONAL FOREST

This forest located in northeastern Arizona, near the town of Holbrook has plenty to keep you busy. The forest is known for fossils petrified in the natural wood, hence named Petrified National Forest. Hike its trails, go backpacking or hop on a horse and ride. Geocaching is another popular activity in this area.

Keep the season in mind before you head over though. Summer temperatures are near 100 degreed Fahrenheit, while winter temperatures are well below freezing. The Painted Desert, Onyx Bridge and

Devil's Playground are just some of the detours you can take on this trip.

17. STRAWBERRY SCHOOLHOUSE MUSEUM

Ever wonder how classrooms looked in the old days? The Strawberry Schoolhouse Museum, which has boasting right to be the oldest standing schoolhouse in Arizona, is located in the town of Strawberry, in Gila County. Although the interior has been completely restored with furniture and chalkboard, the original log frame still stands.

The one building, one room schoolhouse will take you back. Beautifully crafted benches and desks like those used by children back in the day are lined up in classroom fashion. If you have children that are defined by their smartphones and tablets, a visit to the Strawberry Schoolhouse Museum may prove humbling for them. Call ahead, as this school is not open all year-round.

18. LOOK TO THE STARS AT MOUNT GRAHAM INTERNATIONAL OBSERVATORY

The Mt. Graham International Observatory (MGIO) is a collection of telescopes located on the edge of Coronado National Forest used for research in astronomy. The best way to reach the telescopes is through a guided tour that features a scenic trip up Mt. Graham. On this tour, you can witness diverse wildlife, history, and geology of the mountain. Tours up Mt. Graham are offered from mid-May to mid-November, on weekends only. Reservations need to be made in advance.

Amongst other telescopes, the MGIO is also home to the Large Binocular Telescope. Considered to be one of the largest telescopes in the world, this $120 million-dollar telescope takes pictures of the galaxies and universes that surrounds us. Located in southeastern Arizona, this telescope lies on the Tucson campus of the University of Arizona.

19. BEWARE OF PUMPKIN SPRING POOL

It sounds like a swimming pool full of floating pumpkins. However, don't be fooled. Disguising itself in the form of a giant, flooding pumpkin, this pool is home to the most poisonous waters in the Grand Canyon. At mile marker 212 of the Colorado river, the orange walls of this limestone formation, with dirty green water slowing over the edge will undoubtedly remind you of a pumpkin, or a cauldron of sorts. Either way, caution is recommended if you want to take a peek at natural formation.

Although the waters may look warm and welcoming, they are quite the opposite. High levels of arsenic, lead, copper and zinc should be enough to keep you from taking a dip in the green waters. If you want to visit this pool on the Colorado River, a boat is the only way. If you accidentally fall in you should be ok as long as you don't linger. This is not where you would want to work on your tan. Personally, I would not chance it. Long term exposure to these waters is a bad idea for swimming or drinking.

20. UNDERGROUND SUITE, PEACH SPRINGS GRAND CANYON CAVERNS

What is there not to like about a lodging facility in the Grand Canyon. This cavern is 220 feet below canyon grounds, and it is yours to rent for a night. So quiet that you can only hear the sound of your breath, and so dark that you cannot see your own hand in front of your face might scare some away from spending a night here. After all, it is known as Arizona's deepest, darkest hotel room. Plus, it has zero humidity, so there are no other living things to ruin your day.

It's open 364 days a year and is simply a 22-story elevator ride below the ground, a great way to spend the night. Inquire into the price ahead of time. Staying in Peach Springs comes with a price tag and reservations must be made well in advance.

21. VIC & WENDY'S HOT SAUCE COLLECTION, MUSEUM, SANTUM, GALLERY & SHRINE

If you are not a fan of hot sauce, you may not appreciate this collection, but if you like the spice you won't want to miss a chance to visit Vic & Wendy's Hot Sauce Collection, Museum, Santum, Gallery & Shrine located in Glendale, Arizona. Imagine walls lined bottles of hot sauce, from top to bottom. With over 8000 unique bottles of hot sauce from all around the world, Vic and Wendy have the largest private hot sauce collection in the world.

While some of the bottles are autographed, others are from companies that are no longer in business and several are a rare find. This is definitely a museum unique to only Arizona. You will not be able to see a library of hot sauce such as this anywhere else. Just another quirky place to see. I wonder if he stores a bottle of Taco Bell mild, hot or fire sauce.

22. DISCOVER AN UNDERGROUND LAKE IN CAVE OF THE BELLS

If you enjoy cave exploration, a beautiful underground lake lies hidden away in the Cave of the Bells in Southern Arizona. Water in the lake remains at 76 degrees Fahrenheit. The cave is located in a remote location in Sawmill Canyon and can only be accessed by dirt roads. You will need a vehicle capable of traversing rugged terrain in order to reach the entrance to the cave. Not only is the entrance to the cave locked, it is also 10 feet below ground. So be prepared to show of your rope knotting skills in order to descend to the entrance.

Make a reservation ahead of time and get a permit at the Forest Supervisor's Office. They will provide you with a set of keys to unlock the cave. I recommend you take flashlight, rope and a headlamp. I would not put this cave on the list of things to do with the entire family, but for the ones that are physically able, it will be an adventure.

23. WATCH AN OLD-FASHIONED SHOOTOUT AT THE O.K. CORRAL

In 1881, Tombstone, Arizona was the scene of the infamous shootout between Earps known as "the lawmen", and the Clanton-McClaury gang known as "the Cowboys". Visitors can watch daily reenactments of the gunfight, portrayed by actors, on the streets of the Tombstone theater. The O.K. Corral is a great place for visitors and history buffs that are into an old-fashioned show down.

While there, you may also want to stop at the 1880s museum of the Epitaph, Arizona's oldest newspaper. Read all about the gunfight and learn how newspapers were printed back then. Learn more about the assassination of Morgan Earp and the silver boom, which drew crowds to Tombstone. This site is closed on Thanksgiving Day and Christmas.

24. HER SECRET IS PATIENCE

What happens when a team of engineers, architects and designers come together? Multi-dimensional art is created. Although it's not your traditional piece of art on a paper canvas, spectators travel to see this 145 ft. tall aerial sculpture of created by Janet Echelman in 2009, and located in downtown Phoenix.

If you visit this sculpture during the day you will not be able to experience the full effect of the lights swaying in the night sky in response to supposed desert winds. However, you will be able to see the shadow art created on the ground and surrounding establishments. Computer programming and colored lighting provide an illusion that is captivating to the eye.

25. SHOOT VIRTUAL TARGETS AT MODERN ROUND

This virtual shooting lounge is a great place to unwind, have some drinks, enjoy good appetizers, foods and dessert, all while shooting virtual targets on the big screen. The portobello fries, mac and cheese balls and crème brûlée were delicious. I visited this establishment with husband, tween and teens.

There are various shooting scenarios to choose from and with diverse difficulty levels. Players can try their luck with virtual handguns or assault rifles. My tween child was able to keep up with shooting targets in the shape of nonliving objects. For an extra price, your entire party gets the option to choose from law enforcement and military scenarios. Keep in mind that the language in those scenarios is not for young ears. We all enjoyed ourselves and welcomed a unique experience.

26. BRING OUT YOUR INNER CHILD AT LEGOLAND DISCOVERY CENTER

Legos! Legos! Legos everywhere! Just like many other children, I loved playing with Legos as a kid. That is why I appreciate Legoland, where Legos are all over the place, even on the floor. Wear shoes with thick soles so you do not hurt yourself and build away. This attraction best captivates children under 10. You might find your tweens and teens rolling their eyes a bit.

Since it is not as large, it is not as overwhelming as Legoland in California. So you can get your money's worth. Sea Life Aquarium is next door, so if your trip is planned in advance, you might be able to find a combo pass that provides entry to both attractions and save some money on admission fees.

27. APPRECIATE THE HISTORY OF THE APACHE DEATH CAVE

Even though it is a gruesome part of history, the Apache Death Cave is a unique spot that tourists venture out to visit. Located in Winslow, Arizona, this mass grave tells a tale of revenge. A group of Apache believed to have raided a Navajo camp, killing most of the men, women and children, and kidnapping Apache girls, hid out in the underground cave. The Navajos caught up with them and took revenge. They blocked the cave entrance with fire, trapping and killing almost all of the Apache inside.

Parts of the caves are very dark and narrow and rock slides makes sections of it hard to get to. Hiking shoes, or closed-toes sneakers with support are recommended. Local tribes believe the area is cursed and will avoid venturing to it. They might also warn visitors to stay away. If you dare, although not well maintained, the cave is still open.

28. CATCH THE SUNRISE AT MONUMENT VALLEY

If you are looking for a place to catch the sunrise head to Monument Valley National Tribal Park on the Arizona/Utah border. The towering sandstone towers that seem untouched by technology and modern times are admirable.

There are many scenic drives that you can take if you want a self-guided tour. Hiking trails ranging in difficulty level are also an option. You can also hire a local Navajo guide for a jeep outing or a tour on horseback to some of the most recognizable landmarks used as backdrops in numerous Hollywood films. Restaurants serving Navajo cuisine are located in the area in case you get hungry.

29. METEOR CRATER

It may not be the site of the collision that drove the dinosaurs to extinction, but this gigantic crater made by a meteor that crashed with the earth over 50,000 years ago is about 1 mile in diameter. This is a wonderful place to visit with the entire family. Children and adults are left in awe, pondering the power of celestial objects, and can see first hand how they impact our planet.

If you want to walk to the rim of Meteor Crater in northern Arizona, it's best to pack a jacket and pick a day with low winds. Guided tours will take you to the rim of the crater, but the walk is not recommended if the winds are high. The visitor center does a decent job of educating tourists on the history of the crater and providing facts. The air-conditioned theater plays an educational documentary on the subject that is short and informative.

30. GRAND CANYON MULE RIDE

You've seen it in brochures and scenes of movies, but a Grand Canyon mule ride is not for everyone. Riding a mule down the Grand Canyon is an exercise in trust. If you trust those four-legged animals to carry your weight while you are near the edge of cliffs, this experience is for you.

Catch a mule from the North Rim or the South Rim of the canyon. Depending on which you choose rides can last anywhere from one hour to ½ day. Reservations may be made up to 15 months in advance so some planning will be required for this excursion. Once there, visitors will have many opportunities to capture the beautiful scenery in photographs.

31. FLINTSTONES BEDROCK CITY

Meet the Flintstones in Bedrock city! Come visit this theme park and be taken back in time to Saturday morning cartoons. Admission is cheap and you will recognize buildings shown in the cartoon such as the post office, police station and beauty parlor where Betty Rubble and Wilma Flintstone spent some of their time. Ride the Fredmobile tram or catch the cartoons that started is all in the Bedrock Theater.

Some of the sites are a bit run down, but it's a small stop on memory lane. Pick up some mementos in the gift shop or have some snacks while nostalgia takes over. If there are people in your party that did not watch the cartoon as children, they may not appreciate the references and similarities.

32. BUTTERFLY WONDERLAND

With over 3000 butterflies, this is the largest butterfly conservatory in the United States. Located in Scottsdale, Arizona, this attraction explores the life of a butterfly from caterpillar to chrysalis. Equipped with a 3D theater, you can learn everything you want about butterflies at Butterfly Wonderland.

This conservatory is not only limited to Butterflies. There is also a Rainforest Reptile exhibit where visitors can meet some creepy crawlies. If you have the stomach for it, there is also an edible insect station which allows you to sample cuisine such as chocolate covered ants and scorpion lollipops.

The Butterfly Wonderland is just one of the five attractions at the Odysea in the Desert.

33. TAKE A HOUSEBOAT ONTO LAKE POWELL

This beautiful lake is located between Arizona and Utah. There are plenty of opportunities for hiking and fishing. You can even rent a houseboat for the duration of your trip. There are many locations that will rent boats, but prices are high and reservations need to be made in advance, especially during peak vacationing season. We attempted to visit Lake Powell one year in July, but the houseboats were booked since it was a holiday weekend.

Even if you cannot get out on a boat the view of the starry night sky is usually unobstructed. There are also many scenic drives, hiking trails and fishing holes. If you want to take a dip in its clear waters, you might want to visit in the summer months when the waters are warmer. Personally, I enjoy travelling when there are less crowds. Therefore, September is my pick of the best time of year to visit. A great destination for the whole family with plenty to keep everyone busy.

34. VALLEY OF THE MOON

Valley of the Moon is a very unique and peculiar structure in Tucson. It contains a miniature fairy castle, Enchanted Garden and its own wizards tower. Plays are performed here year-round. There are games for kids and even the opportunity to dress up as mystical creatures. Often advertised as a fairyland for children, this attraction was the imagination of George Legler.

Built in the 1920s, Legler wanted this to be a place where messages of kindness and could be spread to all visitors. Tourists and artists often come here to gain a little bit of peace. The attraction is currently zoned as a historic landmark. It may not be the most popular attraction to visit, but it is a quaint little place.

35. SUNRISE PARK RESORT IN THE WHITE MOUNTAINS

Many tourists travel to the White Mountains during the winter to enjoy skiing and other winter sports. Located on Native American land, Sunrise Park Resort is one place where you can stay and be close enough to the activities offered in the area. Ski lessons are available if you want to take your chance on the downhill ski slopes. Snowboarding, sledding and ice-fishing are also other options.

However, winter is not the only time to visit Sunrise Ski Resort. I decided to head up there during the summer time in order to escape the Scottsdale heat. The summer weather at the resort was considerably more comfortable than in Scottsdale. Crowds are scarce at this time of year. Staying at the resort is convenient, however, there is no air-conditioning. If you are driving there you might want to pack a fan.

You can enjoy ziplining, horseback riding and some quality time on the bungee trampoline without too much preplanning. The ski lifts still operate in the summer time. You can take the lift to the top of the mountain, sit down and grab something to eat at the restaurant overlooking the mountains, and then take the lift back down. Take a light jacket as the temperatures at the top are much cooler than those at the bottom.

36. HOOVER DAM

I was trying to describe this engineering marvel to my children who had never visited. All I had to say was "remember, where the dam where they hid Megatron in the first Transformers movie?". They instantly knew what I was talking about. Although there are no Decepticons inside, the Hoover Dam is worth visiting.

Completed in 1935, this dam links Arizona and Nevada and is on the border of the two states. The dam was constructed for the purpose of providing water and hydroelectric power to states in the Southwest. There are worthwhile attractions on both sides of the border. Visitors can drive across the dam, walk across it and even take a tour of the powerplant. Parking on the Arizona side is free, but dam tour tickets are on a first come first serve basis. During peak season and holidays, tourists can expect longer wait times to enter the facility. If you want to learn a bit more about the history of the dam you can visit the Hoover Dam Museum.

37. VISIT THE RUINS OF JEROME

Major cities such as Phoenix, Tucson and Scottsdale are most popular for Arizona tourists, but I prefer the one of a kind little towns. The town of Jerome is located in the Black Hills of the Yavapai County, between Flagstaff and Prescott. It used to be an old copper mining town that flourished during WWI. Now you can visit remnants of the old town.

If mining history peaks your interest, this little town has a mining museum that will stratify history buffs, art galleries, and even a sliding jail. The old jailhouse, which was built on a steep hill and keeps sliding down. It is now over 200 ft away from its original location. If you have more time, do not miss a chance to visit the ruins of the old abandoned post office.

38. COCONINO LAVA RIVER CAVE

Let's face it. Volcanos and lava are just fascinating. Coconino Lava River Cave, located near Flagstaff, in Coconino National Forest was formed by a river of gushing lava, a long time ago. If you are a geologist, this cave will have all sorts of formations to explore such as lava tubes. However, you don't have to be a scientist to appreciate this destination. At about ¾ of a mile long, the cave is suitable for families of all ages to discover.

Due to condensation, surfaces in the cave are slippery so wear proper footwear. Hiking boots or durable gym shoes are my go-to. Temperatures inside the cave are cooler than at the entrance. Some visitors will be alright with long sleeves and pants, but others will find the cave too cold to explore without a jacket. Take flashlights, plenty of water and use the restrooms before you venture out that way, as facilities are limited due to the remote location.

39. TITAN MISSILE MUSEUM

Not every attraction worth visiting in Arizona is hundreds of years old, or built by mother nature. Titan Missile Museum, also known as the Air Force Facility Missile Site 8, is a nuclear missile silo that welcomes tourists. Check out the control room, missiles and living quarters used by former crew members. Located in Green Valley, Arizona, this facility open 1963. A tour through the facility ends with a simulated launch, countdown and blastoff. Do not worry, the missile is not live. This site was decommissioned by President Ronald Reagan. If your heart ¬¬¬¬desires you can even stay over night and experience how it felt to be a crew member, waiting for that signal to launch.

Tours are one-hour long and reservations cannot be made in advance unless you have a large party. There are approximately 55 stair steps that will be taken to and from the site, however the facility is handicapped accessible if needed.

40. POSTINO WINE CAFÉ

I love a place that offers small appetizers and dishes that can be shared over a glass of wine. Postino Wine Café is very popular in the Phoenix area, with multiple locations. This establishment provides the ambiance and food needed for a romantic date night or a good time with friends.

The selection and uniqueness of the bruschetta and boards are enough to keep you coming back. The brie and apple bruschetta with fig spread are one of my favorites. Many vegetarian options such as roasted beets and herbed ricotta, along with soups and salads are also available. If you are interested in a meal that is heavier there are many varieties of panini sandwiches available. With a wide selection of beer and wine your guests will not get bored. You can choose to dine inside, or out by the firepit.

41. 309TH AEROSPACE MAINTENANCE AND REGENERATION GROUP

Where do military aircrafts go when they die? Well they go to the 309th Aerospace Maintenance and Regeneration Group, aka "the boneyard", at Davis-Montham Air Force Base. Here, airplane enthusiasts can pay their respects to almost every type plane flown by the Armed Forces since WWII. Approximately 4000 aircrafts can be found at this location.

However, this is not just a graveyard. Parts from the retired planes are reused in planes that are actually still in service, saving the government and hence the taxpayers, a lot of money. If you want to visit this location and pay homage to the aerospace industry, do not just show up at the gate. You must arrange your tour in advance. The 309th Aerospace Maintenance and Regeneration Group is a great place to visit if you want to learn more about military aviation history.

42. COPPER QUEEN MINE TOUR

In the town of Bisbee, this historic mining tour makes you feel like a real miner. Visitors are provided with a headlamp and hardhat, and board the mine train to descend into the mine. It's not a roller coaster ride, but an informative tour into the abyss of a dark mine. Experience how former miners felt as they descended below ground into the unknown.

Temperatures are chilly, at around 47 degrees Fahrenheit. Warm clothing is recommended. You will have to climb a couple flights of stairs and walk on some uneven ground. So, wear some closed toed shoes and ditch the high heels for this copper mine tour, led by former miners. I would call ahead for tour times and reservations.

43. SATISFY YOUR CRAVINGS AT AKITA SUSHI

If you are in the mood for sushi, Akita Sushi, located in Scottsdale is the place to go. After you arrive, you will be provided with menu and sheets of paper, on which you can write down your order. Here sushi is all you can eat so come prepared with an appetite. The menu is not limited to sushi though.

You will find eggplant and chicken teriyaki dishes, soups, salads, fried rice, udon noodle options and dessert such as green tea ice cream. Again, it is all you can eat! The only rule is you pay for what you waste. My husband children really enjoy the food at Akita. We take our time, order, eat, order some more and repeat. The staff is usually very patient.

The restaurant is located in a standalone facility outside a strip mall. There are plenty of parking spots adjacent to the restaurant. My favorite time to dine at Akita is for a late lunch around 2:30 pm on a Saturday or Sunday. You are charged the all you can eat lunch prices until 4:30, which are close to half of the dinner prices.

44. LONDON BRIDGE IS STILL STANDING

A little-known fact: you do not need to travel to the United Kingdom to visit the London bridge. The original bridge is located in Lake Havasu, Arizona. The bridge was sold to the founder of Lake Havasu City for roughly $2 million dollars. It was carefully dismantled in London in 1967, and then reassembled in Lake Havasu City. Each stone was numbered and then transported by sea to California, then ultimately to Lake Havasu City. Tourists were able to tour the bridge starting in 1971.

The purchase of the bridge was meant to be a publicity stunt with the ultimate goal of putting Lake Havasu on the map. The stunt worked. Lake Havasu City was in headlines all across the world. People still flock there to check out the bridge and learn about its history. Lamps that line the bridge are made from melted cannons that were part of Napoleon's army.

45. MINI TIME MACHINE MUSEUM OF MINIATURES

This gem located in Tucson, Arizona, does not really have that much to do specifically with the history of Arizona. Instead, in its History Gallery, it showcases dollhouses, old and new, depicting life in the 18th, 19th and 20th centuries around the world. The museum's permanent collections include Exploring the World, the Enchanted Realm and History Gallery. The Exploring the World exhibit shows the visitor a little about how miniatures are used in other countries.

If you are into dragons, fairies, fantasy and folklore, do not skip the Enchanted Realm exhibit. Here the most magical miniatures are displayed. In addition to the permanent collection, if you visit during the winter holiday season, you may be able to catch some seasonal exhibits.

Admission to the Mini Time Machine Museum of Miniatures is low-priced as it is, with very reasonable prices for children and youth. Even then, if you stop by a hotel in the area you might be able to save a few bucks on the entrance fee. If you have a large family you might want to look into the family membership. It's a pretty good deal. The museum is not open on Mondays or major holidays.

46. WIGWAM MOTEL

When travelling across the United States, where you stay can sometimes be exciting in itself. Appropriately named, the Wigwam Motel has motel rooms shaped like teepees. I shouldn't need to say more if you are looking for one of a kind. The whole place reminded me of a scene from the Disney's Cars movie. If you want to pull up to a place with vintage cars and feel like you are living in the 50s, this is the stop for you.

Located in the town of Holbrook, AZ, right off of historic Route 66, guests can reserve a night in the teepee-shaped rooms, fully equipped with bathrooms. Staying at the motel will not break the bank, but it is a bit run down. Even if you don't stay here overnight, it is a great place to snap some pictures. This destination is also known as "Wigwam Villages".

47. BIOSPHERE 2

This facility should be renamed heaven for scientists. Managed by the University of Arizona, Biosphere 2 was originally constructed for the purpose of researching and developing technology that would allow for self-colonization in space. Since then, its purpose has evolved to that of scientific research, education and more.

Often referred to as the world's largest science lab, this facility lies in the Santa Catalina Mountains. Visitors can take a tour and experience the different ecosystems. Guided tours are offered daily and require quite a bit of walking and stair climbing. There are some self-guided exhibits that can be viewed on your visit. If those in your party have trouble staying on their feet, I would call ahead to see if some accommodations can be made.

48. SLITHER OVER TO DIAMONDBACK BRIDGE

Named after a venomous rattlesnake, this bridge is actually in the shape of snake and located near downtown Tucson, near Broadway and Euclid. You will not be driving your car across this bridge though as the bridge is for pedestrian and bicycle traffic only. Those traversing the bridge can enter through the snake's head and exit out of the tail. When you get to the other end you used to be able to hear a rattling sound coming from the tail of the bridge. At night time, the snake's eyes also lit up. However, both the rattle and lit eyes no longer work.

This bridge is also known as Rattlesnake Bridge and although it may not a major attraction, it is not a detour that will cost you a lot of time. The bridge is suspended over six lanes of traffic and can be seen from the highway. However, if you do choose to pull over, you can walk across.

49. EMERALD CAVE AND EMERALD COVE

Deep in the Black Canyon you will find Emerald Cave located with Emerald Cove. Book your half-day kayak trip from Willow Beach, Arizona, to Emerald Cove. When you lay your eyes on the tranquil green waters of the Colorado river, you will see that where the destination gets its name.

The sun's reflection, the blue sky and the yellowish-brownish color of the cavern walls combine to give the waters its emerald green color. The round-trip kayak excursion is four miles and local animals, such Desert Bighorn sheep can be seen as your party is led to and from the cove. Call ahead and check temperatures so you are not paddling in high heat.

If kayaking is not your thing, sign up for the three-hour raft tour. Sit on a motorized raft, while your guide takes you and your party to and from the Emerald Cove, Hoover Dam and Willow Beach Gauging Station. Unlike, the kayak or paddle rafts, the motorized raft will not be able to enter Emerald Cave. Wear a hat, sunglasses and ample sunscreen.

50. WRAP IT UP, WITH A TRIP TO THE GRAND CANYON

A trip to Arizona would not be complete without visiting the awe-inspiring Grand Canyon. That is why I couldn't leave it out of this book. This wonder deserves a book of its own. Nothing compares to this stunning creation by mother nature. Every time I visit, I stand in awe, admiring this marvel, carved out by the Colorado River. Camping, hiking, photography, history lessons…you name it. The Grand Canyon has it all.

My advice would be to go on a clear day, otherwise you will end up looking down and seeing only cloud cover, not that cloud cover isn't beautiful. Temperatures at the canyon vary. There could be slick roads and hail up top, requiring you to bundle up in layers, but while on the canyon floor you might prefer shorts and tank tops.

There are many lookout points, where you can pull over and view various parts of the canyon. The sunsets are absolutely amazing. The best views of the canyon vary depending on time of year and weather.

Hopi Point on the South Rim, and Mohave Point just west of it are my favorites.

TOP REASONS TO BOOK THIS TRIP

Landscape: The most beautiful landscapes you will encounter.

History: Various culture and customs are a part of Arizona history.

Weather: Escape the cold, play some golf and enjoy the sun.

OTHER RESOURCES:

https://www.visitarizona.com/planning/travel-tips

http://biosphere2.org/visit/what-is-biosphere-2

https://evolutionexpeditions.com/kayaking/emerald
-cave-kayak.html

https://www.blackcanyonadventures.com/exclusiv
eoffer?gclid=Cj0KCQiAoo7gBRDuARIsANeJKU
Y_1h2ynUsUNwGMp8aI1LaKAruGdwuG0Jk0G
LgsMC3ctiz7-iYJtk8aAp3dEALw_wcB

https://www.pinestrawhs.org/schoolhouse.html

BONUS BOOK

50 THINGS TO KNOW ABOUT PACKING LIGHT FOR TRAVEL

PACK THE RIGHT WAY EVERY TIME

AUTHOR: MANIDIPA BHATTACHARYYA

Edited by Melanie Howthorne

ABOUT THE AUTHOR

Manidipa Bhattacharyya is a creative writer and editor, with an
education in English literature and Linguistics. After working in the IT
industry for seven long years she decided to call it quits and follow her
heart instead. Manidipa has been ghost writing, editing, proof reading
and doing secondary research services for many story tellers and article
writers for about three years. She stays in Kolkata, India with her
husband and a busy two year old. In her own time Manidipa enjoys
travelling, photography and writing flash fiction.

Manidipa believes in travelling light and never carries anything that she
couldn't haul herself on a trip. However, travelling with her child
changed the scenario. She seemed to carry the entire world with her for
the baby on the first two trips. But good sense prevailed and she is
again working her way to becoming a light traveler, this time with a
kid.

INTRODUCTION

*He who would travel happily
must travel light.*

-Antoine de Saint-Exupéry

Travel takes you to different places from seas and mountains to deserts and much more. In your travels you get to interact with different people and their cultures. You will, however, enjoy the sights and interact positively with these new people even more, if you are travelling light.

When you travel light your mind can be free from worry about your belongings. You do not have to spend precious vacation time waiting for your luggage to arrive after a long flight. There is be no chance of your bags going missing and the best part is that you need not pay a fee for checked baggage.

People who have mastered this art of packing light will root for you to take only one carry-on, wherever you go. However, many people can find it really hard to pack light. More so if you are travelling with children. Differentiating between "must have" and "just in case" items is the starting point. There will be ample shopping avenues at your destination which are just waiting to be explored.

This book will show you 'packing' in a new 'light' – pun intended – and help you to embrace light packing practices for all of your future travels.

Off to packing!

DEDICATION

I dedicate this book to all the travel buffs that I know, who have given me great insights into the contents of their backpacks.

THE RIGHT TRAVEL GEAR

1. CHOOSE YOUR TRAVEL GEAR CAREFULLY

While selecting your travel gear, pick items that are light weight, durable and most importantly, easy to carry. There are cases with wheels so you can drag them along – these are usually on the heavy side because of the trolley. Alternatively a backpack that you can carry comfortably on your back, or even a duffel bag that you can carry easily by hand or sling across your body are also great options. Whatever you choose, one thing to keep in mind is that the luggage itself should not weigh a ton, this will give you the flexibility to bring along one extra pair of shoes if you so desire.

2. CARRY THE MINIMUM NUMBER OF BAGS

Selecting light weight luggage is not everything. You need to restrict the number of bags you carry as well. One carry-on size bag is ideal for light travel. Most carriers allow one cabin baggage plus one purse, handbag or camera bag as long as it slides under the seat in front. So technically, you can carry two items of luggage without checking them in.

3. PACK ONE EXTRA BAG

Always pack one extra empty bag along with your essential items. This could be a very light weight duffel bag or even a sturdy tote bag which takes up minimal space. In the event that you end up buying a lot of souvenirs, you already have a handy bag to stuff all that into and do not have to spend time hunting for an appropriate bag.

I'm very strict with my packing and have everything in its right place. I never change a rule. I hardly use anything in the hotel room. I wheel my own wardrobe in and that's it.

Charlie Watts

CLOTHES & ACCESSORIES

4. PLAN AHEAD

Figure out in advance what you plan to do on your trip. That will help you to pick that one dress you need for the occasion. If you are going to attend a wedding then you have to carry formal wear. If not, you can ditch the gown for something lighter that will be comfortable during long walks or on the beach.

5. WEAR THAT JACKET

Remember that wearing items will not add extra luggage for your air travel. So wear that bulky jacket that you plan to carry for your trip. This saves space and can also help keep you warm during the chilly flight.

6. MIX AND MATCH

Carry clothes that can be interchangeably used to reinvent your look. Find one top that goes well with a couple of pairs of pants or skirts. Use tops, shirts and jackets wisely along with other accessories like a scarf or a stole to create a new look.

7. CHOOSE YOUR FABRIC WISELY

Stuffing clothes in cramped bags definitely takes its toll which results in wrinkles. It is best to carry wrinkle free, synthetic clothes or merino tops. This will eliminate the need for that small iron you usually bring along.

8. DITCH CLOTHES PACK UNDERWEAR

Pack more underwear and socks. These are the things that will give you a fresh feel even if you do not get a chance to wear fresh clothes. Moreover these are easy to wash and can be dried inside the hotel room itself.

9. CHOOSE DARK OVER LIGHT

While picking your clothes choose dark coloured ones. They are easy to colour coordinate and can last longer before needing a wash. Accidental food spills and dirt from the road are less visible on darker clothes.

10. WEAR YOUR JEANS

Take only one pair of Jeans with you, which you should wear on the flight. Remember to pick a pair that can be worn for sightseeing trips and is equally

71

eloquent for dinner. You can add variety by adding light weight cargoes and chinos.

11. CARRY SMART ACCESSORIES

The right accessory can give you a fresh look even with the same old dress. An intelligent neck-piece, a couple of bright scarves, stoles or a sarong can be used in a number of ways to add variety to your clothing. These light weight beauties can double up as a nursing cover, a light blanket, beach wear, a modesty cover for visiting places of worship, and also makes for an enthralling game of peek-a-boo.

12. LEARN TO FOLD YOUR GARMENTS

Seasoned travellers all swear by rolling their clothes for compact and wrinkle free packing. Bundle packing, where you roll the clothes around a central object as if tying it up, is also a popular method of compact and wrinkle free packing. Stacking folded clothes one on top of another is a big no-no as it makes creases extreme and they are difficult to get rid of without ironing.

13. WASH YOUR DIRTY LAUNDRY

One of the ways to avoid carrying loads of clothes is to wash the clothes you carry. At some places you might get to use the laundry services or a Laundromat but if you are in a pinch, best solution is to wash them yourself. If that is the plan then carrying quick drying clothes is highly recommended, which most often also happen to be the wrinkle free variety.

14. LEAVE THOSE TOWELS BEHIND

Regular towels take up a lot of space, are heavy and take ages to dry out. If you are staying at hotels they will provide you with towels anyway. If you are travelling to a remote place, where the availability of towels look doubtful, carry a light weight travel towel of viscose material to do the job.

15. USE A COMPRESSION BAG

Compression bags are getting lots of recommendation now days from regular travellers. These are useful for saving space in your luggage when you have to pack bulky dresses. While packing for the return trip, get help from the hotel staff to arrange a vacuum cleaner.

FOOTWEAR

16. PUT ON YOUR HIKING BOOTS

If you have plans to go hiking or trekking during your trip, you will need those bulky hiking boots. The best way to carry them is to wear them on flight to save space and luggage weight. You can remove the boots once inside and be comfortable in your socks.

17. PICKING THE RIGHT SHOES

Shoes are often the bulkiest items, along with being the dainty if you are a female. They need care and take up a lot of space in your luggage. It is advisable therefore to pick shoes very carefully. If you plan to do a lot of walking and site seeing, then wearing a pair of comfortable walking shoes are a must. For more formal occasions you can carry durable, light weight flats which will not take up much space.

18. STUFF SHOES

If you happen to pack a pair of shoes, ensure you utilize their hollow insides. Tuck small items like rolled up socks or belts to save space. They will also be easy to find.

TOILETRIES

19. STASHING TOILETRIES

Carry only absolute necessities. Airline rules dictate
that for one carry-on bag, liquids and gels must be in
3.4 ounce (100ml) bottles or less, and must be packed
in a one quart zip-lock bag. If you are planning to stay
in a hotel, the basic things will be provided for you.
It's best is to buy the rest from the local market at
your destination.

20. TAKE ALONG TAMPONS

Tampons are a hard to find item in a lot of countries.
Figure out how many you need and pack accordingly.
For longer stays you can buy them online and have
them delivered to where you are staying.

21. GET PAMPERED BEFORE
YOU TRAVEL

Some avid travellers suggest getting a pedicure and
manicure just the day before travelling. This not only
gives you a well kept look, you also save the trouble
of packing nail polish. Remember, every little bit of
weight reduced adds up.

ELECTRONICS

22. LUGGING ALONG ELECTRONICS

Electronics have a large role to play in our lives today. Most of us cannot imagine our lives away from our phones, laptops or tablets. However while travelling, one must consider the amount of weight these electronics add to our luggage. Thankfully smart phones come along with all the essentials tools like a camera, email access, picture editing tools and more. They are smart to the point of eliminating the need to carry multiple gadgets. Choose a smart phone that suits all your requirements and travel with the world in your palms or pocket.

23. REDUCE THE NUMBER OF CHARGERS

If you do travel with multiple electronic devices, you will have to bear the additional burden of carrying all their chargers too. Check if a single charger can be used for multiple devices. You might also consider investing in a pocket charger. These small devices support multiple devices while keeping you charged on the go.

24. TRAVEL FRIENDLY APPS

Along with smart phones come numerous apps, which are immensely helpful in our travels. You name it and you have an app for it at hand – take pictures, sharing with friends and family, torch to light dark roads, maps, checking flight/train times, find hotels and many other things. Use these smart alternatives to traditional items like books to eliminate weight and save space.

I get ideas about what's essential when packing my suitcase.

-Diane von Furstenberg

TRAVELLING WITH KIDS

25. BRING ALONG THE STROLLER

Kids might enjoy walking for a while but they soon tire out and a stroller is the just the right thing for them to rest in while you continue your tour. Strollers also double duty as a luggage carrier and shopping bag holder. Remember to pick a light weight, easy to handle brand of stroller. Better yet, find out in advance if you can rent a stroller at your destination.

26. BRING ONLY ENOUGH DIAPERS FOR YOUR TRIP

Diapers take up a lot of space and add to the weight of your luggage. Therefore it is advisable to carry just enough diapers to last through the trip and a few for afterwards, till you buy fresh stock at your destination. Unless of course you are travelling to a really remote area, in which case you have no choice but to carry the load. Otherwise diapers are something you will find pretty easily.

27. TAKE ONLY A COUPLE OF TOYS

Children are easily attracted by new things in their environment. While travelling they will find numerous 'new' objects to scrutinize and play with. Packing just one favorite toy is enough, or if there is no favorite toy leave out all of them in favor of stories or imaginary games.

28. CARRY KID FRIENDLY SNACKS

Create a small snack counter in your bag to store away quick bites for those sudden hunger pangs. Depending on the child's age this could include chocolates, raisins, dry fruits, granola bars or biscuits. Also keep a bottle of water handy for your little one.

These things do not add much weight and can be adjusted in a handbag or knapsack.

29. GAMES TO CARRY

Create some travel specific, imaginary games if you have slightly grown up children, like spot the attractions. Keep a coloring book and colors handy for in-flight or hotel time. Apps on your smart phone can keep the children engaged with cartoons and story books. Older children are often entertained by games available on phones or tablets. This cuts the weight of luggage down while keeping the kids entertained.

30. LET THE KIDS CARRY THEIR LOAD

A good thing is to start early sharing of responsibilities. Let your child pick a bag of his or her choice and pack it themselves. Keep tabs on what they are stuffing in their bags by asking if they will be using that item on the trip. It could start out being just an entertainment bag initially but with growing years they will learn to sort the useful from the superfluous. Children as little as four can maneuver a small trolley suitcase like a pro- their experience in pull along toys credit. If you are worried that you may be pulling it for them, you may want to start with a backpack.

31. DECIDE ON LOCATION FOR CHILDREN TO SLEEP

While on a trip you might not always get a crib at your destination, and carrying one will make life all the more difficult. Instead call ahead to see if there are any cribs or roll out beds for children. You may even put blankets on the floor. Weave them a story about camping and they will gladly sleep without any trouble.

32. GET BABY PRODUCTS DELIVERED AT YOUR DESTINATION

If you are absolutely paranoid about not getting your favourite variety of diaper or brand of baby food, check out online stores like amazon.com for services in your destination city. You can buy things online ahead of your travel and get them delivered to your hotel upon arrival.

33. FEEDING NEEDS OF YOUR INFANTS

If you are travelling with a breastfed infant, you save the trouble of carrying bottles and bottle sanitization kits. For special food, or medications, you may need to call ahead to make sure you have a refrigerator where you are staying.

34. FEEDING NEEDS OF YOUR TODDLER

With the progression from infancy to toddler, their dietary requirements too evolve. You will have to pack some snacks for travelling time. Fresh fruits and vegetables can be purchased at your destination. Most of the cities you travel to in whichever part of the world, will have baby food products and formulas, available at the local drug-store or the supermarket.

35. PICKING CLOTHES FOR YOUR BABY

Contrary to popular belief, babies can do without many changes of clothes. At the most pack 2 outfits per day. Pack mix and match type clothes for your little one as well. Pick things which are comfortable to wear and quick to dry.

36. SELECTING SHOES FOR YOUR BABY

Like outfits, kids can make do with two pairs of comfortable shoes. If you can get some water resistant shoes it will be best. To expedite drying wet shoes, you can stuff newspaper in them then wrap them with newspaper and leave them to dry overnight.

37. KEEP ONE CHANGE OF CLOTHES HANDY

Travelling with kids can be tricky. Keep a change of clothes for the kids and mum handy in your purse or tote bag. This takes a bit of space in your hand luggage but comes extremely handy in case there are any accidents or spills.

38. LEAVE BEHIND BABY ACCESSORIES

Baby accessories like their bed, bath tub, car seat, crib etc. should be left at home. Many hotels provide a crib on request, while car seats can be borrowed from friends or rented. Babies can be given a bath in the hotel sink or even in the adult bath tub with a little bit of water. If you bring a few bath toys, they can be used in the bath, pool, and out of water. They can also be sanitized easily in the sink.

39. CARRY A SMALL LOAD OF PLASTIC BAGS

With children around there are chances of a number of soiled clothes and diapers. These plastic bags help to sort the dirt from the clean inside your big bag.

These are very light weight and come in handy to other carry stuff as well at times.

PACK WITH A PURPOSE

40. PACKING FOR BUSINESS TRIPS

One neutral-colored suit should suffice. It can be paired with different shirts, ties and accessories for different occasions. One pair of black suit pants could be worn with a matching jacket for the office or with a snazzy top for dinner.

41. PACKING FOR A CRUISE

Most cruises have formal dinners, and that formal dress usually takes up a lot of space. However you might find a tuxedo to rent. For women, a short black dress with multiple accessory options will do the trick.

42. PACKING FOR A LONG TRIP OVER DIFFERENT CLIMATES

The secret packing mantra for travel over multiple climates is layering. Layering traps air around your body creating insulation against the cold. The same light t-shirt that is comfortable in a warmer climate can be the innermost layer in a colder climate.

REDUCE SOME MORE WEIGHT

43. LEAVE PRECIOUS THINGS AT HOME

Things that you would hate to lose or get damaged leave them at home. Precious jewelry, expensive gadgets or dresses, could be anything. You will not require these on your trip. Leave them at home and spare the load on your mind.

44. SEND SOUVENIRS BY MAIL

If you have spent all your money on purchasing souvenirs, carrying them back in the same bag that you brought along would be difficult. Either pack everything in another bag and check it in the airport or get everything shipped to your home. Use an international carrier for a secure transit, but this could be more expensive than the checking fees at the airport.

45. AVOID CARRYING BOOKS

Books equal to weight. There are many reading apps which you can download on your smart phone or tab.

Plus there are gadgets like Kindle and Nook that are thinner and lighter alternatives to your regular book.

CHECK, GET, SET, CHECK AGAIN

46. STRATEGIZE BEFORE PACKING

Create a travel list and prepare all that you think you need to carry along. Keep everything on your bed or floor before packing and then think through once again – do I really need that? Any item that meets this question can be avoided. Remove whatever you don't really need and pack the rest.

47. TEST YOUR LUGGAGE

Once you have fully packed for the trip take a test trip with your luggage. Take your bags and go to town for window shopping for an hour. If you enjoy your hour long trip it is good to go, if not, go home and reduce the load some more. Repeat this test till you hit the right weight.

48. ADD A ROLL OF DUCT TAPE

You might wonder why, when this book has been talking about reducing stuff, we're suddenly asking you to pack something totally unusual. This is because when you have limited supplies, duct tape is immensely helpful for small repairs – a broken bag, leaking zip-lock bag, broken sunglasses, you name it and duct tape can fix it, temporarily.

49. LIST OF ESSENTIAL ITEMS

Even though the emphasis is on packing light, there are things which have to be carried for any trip. Here is our list of essentials:

•Passport/Visa or any other ID

•Any other paper work that might be required on a trip like permits, hotel reservation confirmations etc.

•Medicines – all your prescription medicines and emergency kit, especially if you are travelling with children

•Medical or vaccination records

•Money in foreign currency if travelling to a different country

•Tickets- Email or Message them to your phone

50. MAKE THE MOST OF YOUR TRIP

Wherever you are going, whatever you hope to do we encourage you to embrace it whole-heartedly. Take in the scenery, the culture and above all, enjoy your time away from home.

On a long journey even a straw weighs heavy.

-Spanish Proverb

PACKING AND PLANNING TIPS

A Week before Leaving

- Arrange for someone to take care of pets and water plants.

- Stop mail and newspaper.

- Notify Credit Card companies where you are going.

- Change your thermostat settings.

- Car inspected, oil is changed, and tires have the correct pressure.

- Passports and photo identification is up to date.

- Pay bills.

- Copy important items and download travel Apps.

- Start collecting small bills for tips.

Right Before Leaving

- Clean out refrigerator.

- Empty garbage cans.

- Lock windows.

- Make sure you have the proper identification with you.

- Bring cash for tips.

- Remember travel documents.

- Lock door behind you.

- Remember wallet.

- Unplug items in house and pack chargers.

>TOURIST

READ OTHER
GREATER THAN A TOURIST
BOOKS

Greater Than a Tourist San Miguel de Allende Guanajuato Mexico:
50 Travel Tips from a Local by Tom Peterson

Greater Than a Tourist – Lake George Area New York USA:
 50 Travel Tips from a Local by Janine Hirschklau

Greater Than a Tourist – Monterey California United States:
50 Travel Tips from a Local by Katie Begley

 Greater Than a Tourist – Chanai Crete Greece:
50 Travel Tips from a Local by Dimitra Papagrigoraki

Greater Than a Tourist – The Garden Route Western Cape Province
South Africa: 50 Travel Tips from a Local by Li-Anne McGregor van
Aardt

Greater Than a Tourist – Sevilla Andalusia Spain:
50 Travel Tips from a Local by Gabi Gazon

Greater Than a Tourist – Kota Bharu Kelantan Malaysia:
50 Travel Tips from a Local by Aditi Shukla

Children's Book: Charlie the Cavalier Travels the World by Lisa
Rusczyk

>TOURIST

> TOURIST

Visit Greater Than a Tourist for Free Travel Tips
http://GreaterThanATourist.com

Sign up for the Greater Than a Tourist Newsletter for discount days, new books, and travel information:
http://eepurl.com/cxspyf

Follow us on Facebook for tips, images, and ideas:
https://www.facebook.com/GreaterThanATourist

Follow us on Pinterest for travel tips and ideas:
http://pinterest.com/GreaterThanATourist

Follow us on Instagram for beautiful travel images:
http://Instagram.com/GreaterThanATourist

>TOURIST

> TOURIST

Please leave your honest review of this book on Amazon and Goodreads. Please send your feedback to GreaterThanaTourist@gmail.com as we continue to improve the series. We appreciate your positive and constructive feedback. Thank you.

METRIC CONVERSIONS

TEMPERATURE

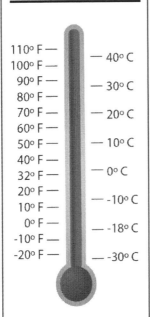

110° F —
100° F — — 40° C
90° F —
80° F — — 30° C
70° F —
60° F — — 20° C
50° F — — 10° C
40° F —
32° F — — 0° C
20° F —
10° F — — -10° C
0° F — — -18° C
-10° F —
-20° F — — -30° C

To convert F to C:

Subtract 32, and then multiply by 5/9 or .5555.

To Convert C to F:

Multiply by 1.8 and then add 32.

32F = 0C

LIQUID VOLUME

To Convert:..................Multiply by
U.S. Gallons to Liters................ 3.8
U.S. Liters to Gallons 26
Imperial Gallons to U.S. Gallons 1.2
Imperial Gallons to Liters....... 4.55
Liters to Imperial Gallons 22
1 Liter = .26 U.S. Gallon
1 U.S. Gallon = 3.8 Liters

DISTANCE

To convert ....Multiply by
Inches to Centimeters 2.54
Centimeters to Inches 39
Feet to Meters....................... .3
Meters to Feet 3.28
Yards to Meters 91
Meters to Yards 1.09
Miles to Kilometers 1.61
Kilometers to Miles............ .62
1 Mile = 1.6 km
1 km = .62 Miles

WEIGHT

1 Ounce = .28 Grams
1 Pound = .4555 Kilograms
1 Gram = .04 Ounce
1 Kilogram = 2.2 Pounds

97

TRAVEL QUESTIONS

- Do you bring presents home to family or friends after a vacation?

- Do you get motion sick?

- Do you have a favorite billboard?

- Do you know what to do if there is a flat tire?

- Do you like a sun roof open?

- Do you like to eat in the car?

- Do you like to wear sun glasses in the car?

- Do you like toppings on your ice cream?

- Do you use public bathrooms?

- Did you bring your cell phone and does it have power?

- Do you have a form of identification with you?

- Have you ever been pulled over by a cop?

- Have you ever given money to a stranger on a road trip?

- Have you ever taken a road trip with animals?

- Have you ever went on a vacation alone?

- Have you ever run out of gas?

- If you could move to any place in the world, where would it be?

- If you could travel anywhere in the world, where would you travel?

- If you could travel in any vehicle, which one would it be?

- If you had three things to wish for from a magic genie, what would they be?

- If you have a driver's license, how many times did it take you to pass the test?

- What are you the most afraid of on vacation?

- What do you want to get away from the most when you are on vacation?

- What foods smells bad to you?

- What item do you bring on ever trip with you away from home?

- What makes you sleepy?

- What song would you love to hear on the radio when you're cruising on the highway?

- What travel job would you want the least?

- What will you miss most while you are away from home?

- What is something you always wanted to try?

- What is the best road side attraction that you ever saw?

- What is the farthest distance you ever biked?

- What is the farthest distance you ever walked?

- What is the weirdest thing you needed to buy while on vacation?

- What is your favorite candy?

- What is your favorite color car?

- What is your favorite family vacation?

- What is your favorite food?

- What is your favorite gas station drink or food?

- What is your favorite license plate design?

- What is your favorite restaurant?

- What is your favorite smell?

- What is your favorite song?

- What is your favorite sound that nature makes?

- What is your favorite thing to bring home from a vacation?

- What is your favorite vacation with friends?

- What is your favorite way to relax?

- Where is the farthest place you ever traveled in a car?

- Where is the farthest place you ever went North, South, East and West?

- Where is your favorite place in the world?

- Who is your favorite singer?

- Who taught you how to drive?

- Who will you miss the most while you are away?

- Who if the first person you will contact when you get to your destination?

- Who brought you on your first vacation?

- Who likes to travel the most in your life?

- Would you rather be hot or cold?

- Would you rather drive above, below, or at the speed limited?

- Would you rather drive on a highway or a back road?

- Would you rather go on a train or a boat?

- Would you rather go to the beach or the woods?

TRAVEL BUCKET LIST

1.

2.

3.

4.

5.

6.

7.

8.

9.

10.

NOTES

Made in the USA
Middletown, DE
18 February 2020